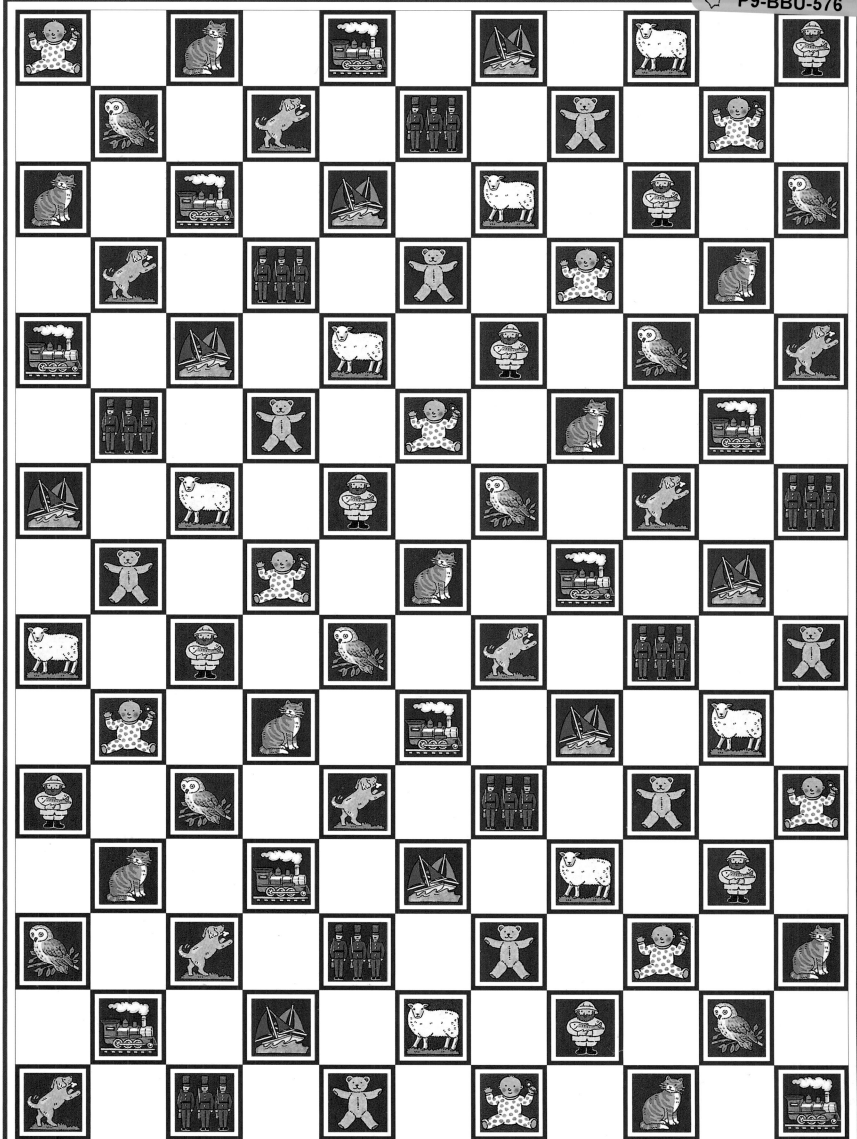

DK

A DORLING KINDERSLEY BOOK

Art Editor Sara Hill
Designer Mary Sandberg
U. S. Editor B. Alison Weir
Production Josie Alabaster

Photography Susanna Price and Paul Bricknell
Illustrations Jane Cradock-Watson
Costumes Barbara Owen

First American Edition, 1993
2 4 6 8 10 9 7 5 3 1

Published in the United States by
Dorling Kindersley, Inc., 232 Madison Avenue
New York, New York 10016

Library of Congress Cataloging-in-Publication Data

Counting rhymes / selected by Shona McKellar. — 1st American ed.
  p. cm
  Summary: A collection of poems, including "One Little Finger," "I
Saw Three Ships Come Sailing By," and "This Old Man," each featuring
different numbers.
  ISBN 1-56458-309-0
  1. Counting—Juvenile poetry. 2. Children's poetry. [1. Poetry—
Collections. 2. Counting.] I. McKellar, Shona.
PN6109.97.C68 1993
398.8'4—dc20   93-12383
                                                        CIP
                                                        AC

Color reproduction by Colourscan, Singapore
Printed in Italy by Graphicom

For permission to reproduce copyright material, the editor and publishers are indebted to:
John Agard c/o Caroline Sheldon Literary Agency for "One Finger Can't Catch Flea" from
Say It Again, Granny! published by The Bodley Head 1986; Charles Causley for "Twenty-four
Hours" from *Jack the Treacle Eater* published by Macmillan; Mr Leland B. Jacobs for
"Eight Witches" by B.J. Lee; John Kitching for "Can't Wait" from *A First Poetry Book*;
Jean Rintoul for "Let's Send a Rocket" by Kit Patrickson from *Poems for Me.*
Every effort has been made to trace the owners of copyright material,
but we take this opportunity of to apologize to any owners
whose rights have been unwittingly infringed.

The publishers would also like to thank the following for their help
in producing this book:
Beadmore, Creative Quilting, Elizabeth David Cookshop, Gamba,
The Garden Centre, Sophisto-cat, Soupdragon at Best of British.

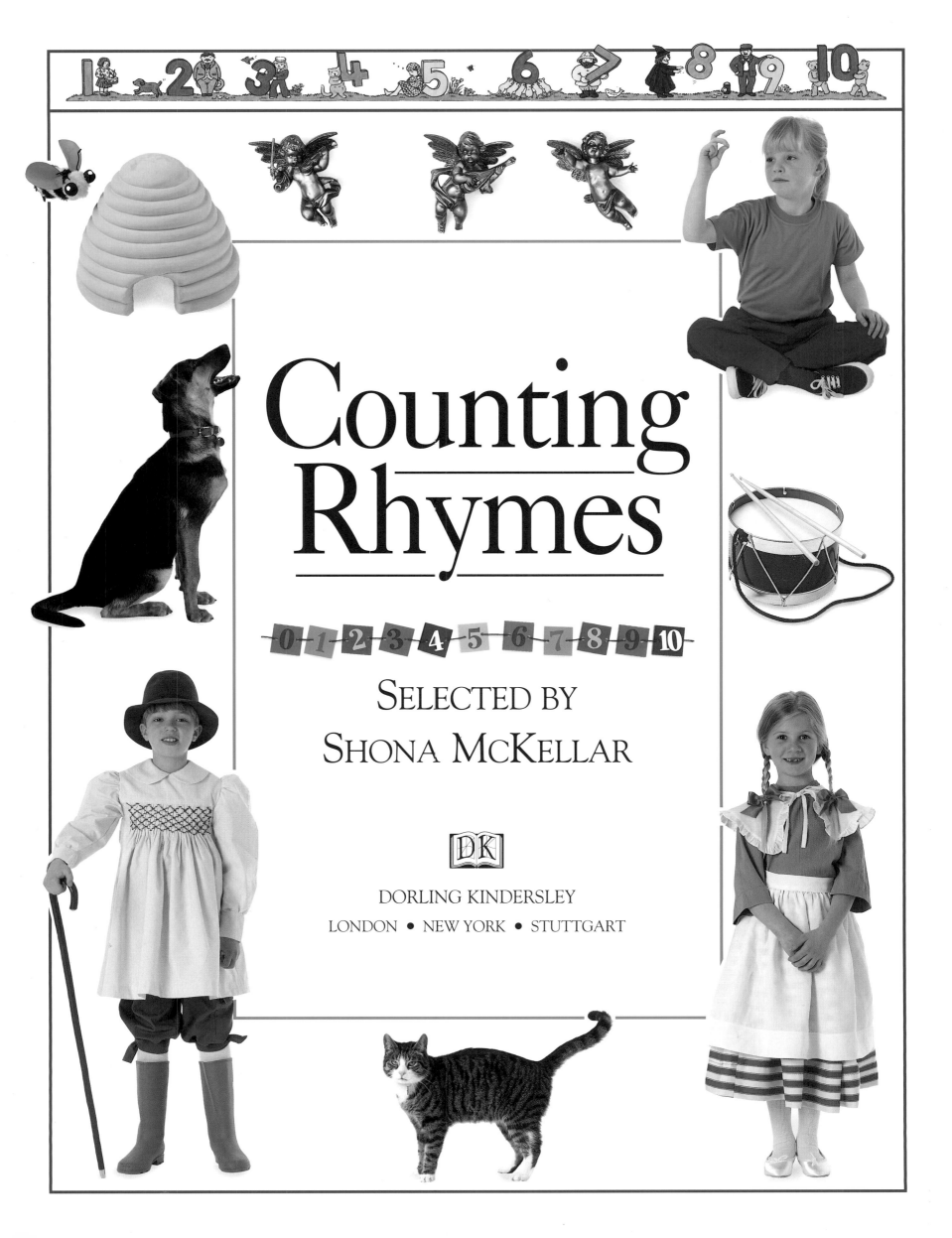

Counting Rhymes

Selected By
Shona McKellar

DK

Dorling Kindersley
LONDON • NEW YORK • STUTTGART

CONTENTS

Wiggle

Tickle

Snap

One finger can wiggle
One finger can tickle.
But have you ever seen
a one-finger snap?

One hand can wave
One hand can flap.
But have you ever seen
a one-hand clap?

Clap

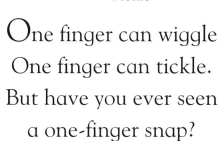

One finger can pat a cat
One finger can stroke a dog.
But I'm sure you'll agree
with my Granny
that one finger can't catch flea.

Wave

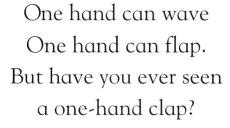

Flap

So let's work together, you and me,
like two hands from one body.

John Agard

Pat

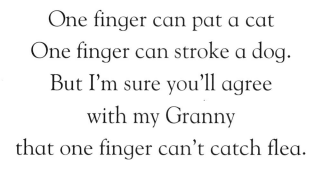

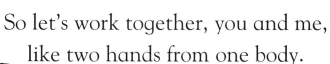

Stroke

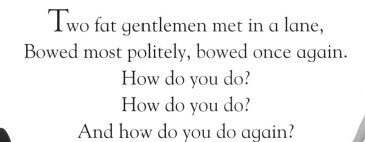

Two fat gentlemen met in a lane,
Bowed most politely, bowed once again.
How do you do?
How do you do?
And how do you do again?

Two thin ladies met in a lane,
Bowed most politely, bowed once again.
How do you do?
How do you do?
And how do you do again?

Two tall mailmen met in a lane,
Bowed most politely, bowed once again.
How do you do?
How do you do?
And how do you do again?

Two little schoolboys met in a lane,
Bowed most politely, bowed once again.
How do you do?
How do you do?
And how do you do again?

Two little babies met in a lane,
Bowed most politely, bowed once again.
How do you do?
How do you do?
And how do you do again?

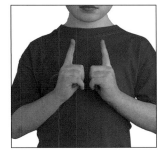

Two fat gentlemen   *Two thin ladies*   *Two tall mailmen*   *Two little schoolboys*   *Two little babies*

3 I SAW THREE SHIPS COME SAILING BY

I saw three ships come sailing by,
Sailing by,
Sailing by,
I saw three ships come sailing by,
On Christmas Day in the morning.

And what do you think was in them then,
Was in them then,
Was in them then?
And what do you think was in them then,
On Christmas Day in the morning?

Three pretty girls were in them then,
Were in them then,
Were in them then,
Three pretty girls were in them then,
On Christmas Day in the morning.

One could whistle and one could sing
And one could play
On the violin.
Such joy there was at my wedding,
On Christmas Day in the morning.

4 THIS MORNING I COUNTED TO FOUR

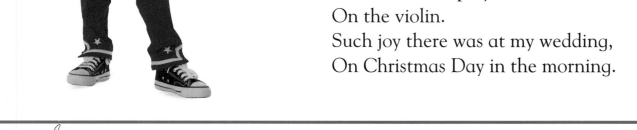

This morning I counted to four:
When the cat jumped on my bed,
1, 2, 3, 4 legs,
When I had my breakfast,
1, 2, 3, 4 chairs,
When I played with my truck,
1, 2, 3, 4 wheels.
And when I went to sleep,
1, 2, 3, 4 . . . .

Five little owls in an old elm tree,
Fluffy and puffy as owls could be.
Blinking and winking with big round eyes
At the big round moon that hung in the skies.
As I passed beneath, I could hear one say,
"There'll be mouse for supper, there will, to-day!"

Then all of them hooted, "Tu-whit, Tu-whoo!
Yes, mouse for supper, Hoo hoo, Hoo hoo!"

11

Six little mice sat down to spin:
Pussy passed by and she peeped in.
  "What are you doing, my little men?"
  "Weaving coats for gentlemen."
    "Shall I come in and cut off your threads?"
    "No, no, Mistress Pussy, you'd bite off our heads."
  "Oh, no, I'll not; I'll help you to spin."
  "That may be so, but you don't come in."

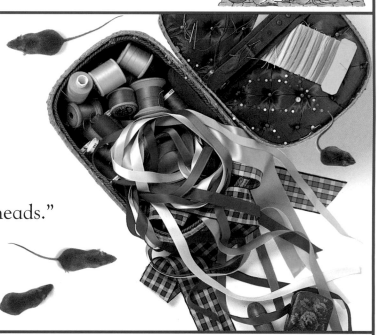

RIDDLE

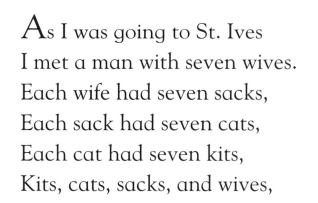

As I was going to St. Ives
I met a man with seven wives.
Each wife had seven sacks,
Each sack had seven cats,
Each cat had seven kits,
Kits, cats, sacks, and wives,
How many were going to St. Ives?

12

Eight witches rode the midnight sky.
One wailed low, and one wailed high.
Another croaked, another sighed
Throughout the eerie midnight ride.

One witch's voice was cackly toned,
Another shrieked, another moaned.
The eighth, much younger than the rest,
Made a scary sound the best —

YOOOO!

YOOOO!

YOOOO!

YOOOO!

B. J. Lee

Engine, engine, number nine,
Sliding down Chicago line.
When she's polished, she will shine,
Engine, engine, number nine.

 # TEN LITTLE TEDDY BEARS

Ten little teddy bears stand up straight,
Ten little teddy bears make a gate.
Ten little teddy bears make a ring,
Ten little teddy bears bow to the king.
Ten little teddy bears dance all day,
Ten little teddy bears hide away.

Stand up straight

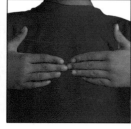

Make a gate

Make a ring

Bow to the king

Dance all day

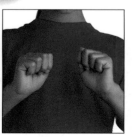

Hide away

Winkle

Tiddler

Tadpole

Cartwheel

Crab

Dab

Eel

Seven fat fishermen,
Sitting side-by-side,
Fished from a bridge,
By the banks of the Clyde.

The first caught a tiddler,
The second caught a crab,
The third caught a winkle,
The fourth caught a dab.

The fifth caught a tadpole,
The sixth caught an eel,
But the seventh, he caught
An old cartwheel.

Not having much fun
At One.

In a cage (like a zoo)
At Two.

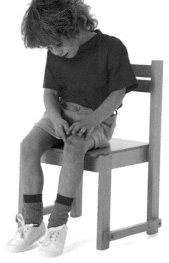

Scraping a knee
At Three.

Ever asking for more
At Four.

Busy bee in a hive
At Five.

Playing war with sticks
At Six.

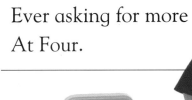

Running is heaven
At Seven.

I can't wait
To be Eight.

John Kitching

1

This old man, he played one,
He played nick-nack on my drum.

Nick-nack paddy whack,
Give a dog a bone,
This old man came rolling home.

2

This old man, he played two,
He played nick-nack on my shoe.

Nick-nack paddy whack,
Give a dog a bone,
This old man came rolling home.

3

This old man, he played three,
He played nick-nack on my knee.

Nick-nack paddy whack,
Give a dog a bone,
This old man came rolling home.

4

This old man, he played four,
He played nick-nack on my door.

Nick-nack paddy whack,
Give a dog a bone,
This old man came rolling home.

5

This old man, he played five,
He played nick-nack on my hive.

Nick-nack paddy whack,
Give a dog a bone,
This old man came rolling home.

6

This old man, he played six,
He played nick-nack on my sticks.

Nick-nack paddy whack,
Give a dog a bone,
This old man came rolling home.

7

This old man, he played seven,
He played nick-nack up in heaven.

Nick-nack paddy whack,
Give a dog a bone,
This old man came rolling home.

8

This old man, he played eight,
He played nick-nack on my plate.

Nick-nack paddy whack,
Give a dog a bone,
This old man came rolling home.

9

This old man, he played nine,
He played nick-nack on my line.

Nick-nack paddy whack,
Give a dog a bone,
This old man came rolling home.

10

This old man, he played ten,
He played nick-nack on my hen.

Nick-nack paddy whack,
Give a dog a bone,
This old man came rolling home.

TWENTY-FOUR HOURS

Twenty-four hours
  Make a night and a day;
Never a minute
  More will one stay.

One o'clock sounds
  To the owl's cold cry;
Two, as the flame of the fox
  Glimmers by.

Three, the still hour
  Of the moon and the star;
Four, the first cockcrow
  Is heard from afar.

Five, and the bird-song
  Already begun;
Six, the bright mail van
  Comes up with the sun.

Seven, here's the milk
  With the butter and cream;
Eight, all the kettles
  Are letting off steam.

Nine, the school bell
  Calls the lazy and late;
Ten, as the children
  Chant, "Two fours are eight."

Eleven, and it's cooking
  With pot, pan, and spoon;
Twelve, and the morning
  Says, "Good afternoon!"

One, and for dinner
  Hot pudding and pie;
Two, all the dishes
  Are watered and dry.

Three, the quick water-hen
  Hides in the pool;
Four, as the children
  Come smiling from school.

Five, see the milking cows
  Lurch down the lane;
Six, and the family
  Together again.

Seven, and the children
  Are bathed and in bed;
Eight, Dad is snoozing
  The paper unread.

Nine, and the house mouse
  Squints out of his hole;
Ten, and the tabby cat
  Takes a dark stroll.

Eleven, bolt the window
  And lock the front door;
Twelve o'clock strikes
  And on sea and on shore
Night and day's journey
  Is starting once more.
Twelve o'clock sounds
  On the steep and the plain,
Day and night's journey
  Beginning again.

Twenty-four hours
  Make a night and a day;
Never a minute
  More will one stay.
Never a moment
  Will one delay.
So much to do
  And so much to say:
Why must they always
  Hurry away?

Charles Causley

One, two,
Buckle my shoe.

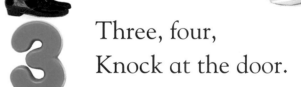

Three, four,
Knock at the door.

Five, six,
Pick up sticks.

Seven, eight,
Lay them straight.

Nine, ten,
A big fat hen.

Eleven, twelve,
Dig and delve.

Thirteen, fourteen,
Maids a-courting.

Fifteen, sixteen,
Maids in the kitchen.

Seventeen, eighteen,
Maids in waiting.

Nineteen, twenty,
My plate's empty!

One *Two* *Three* *Four* *Five*

John Brown had a little soldier,
John Brown had a little soldier,
John Brown had a little soldier,
One little soldier boy.
He had one little, two little, three little soldiers,
Four little, five little, six little soldiers,
Seven little, eight little, nine little soldiers,
Ten little soldier boys.

Hoy!

John Brown had ten little soldiers,
John Brown had ten little soldiers,
John Brown had ten little soldiers,
Ten little soldier boys.
He had ten little, nine little, eight little soldiers,
Seven little, six little, five little soldiers,
Four little, three little, two little soldiers,
One little soldier boy.

Hoy!

Six *Seven* *Eight* *Nine* *Ten*

Two little eyes to look around,
Two little ears to hear each sound,
One little nose to smell what's sweet,
One little mouth that likes to eat.

Two legs sat upon three legs
With one leg in her lap.

In comes four legs
And runs away with one leg.

Up jumps two legs,
Catches up three legs,
Throws it after four legs,
And makes him bring back one leg.

There were five in the bed
and the little one said, "Roll over! Roll over!"
So they all rolled over and one fell out.

There were four in the bed
and the little one said, "Roll over! Roll over!"
So they all rolled over and one fell out.

There were three in the bed
and the little one said, "Roll over! Roll over!"
So they all rolled over and one fell out.

There were two in the bed
and the little one said, "Roll over! Roll over!"
So they all rolled over and one fell out.

There was one in the bed
and the little one said,
"Good, now I've got the bed to myself,
I'm going to stretch and stretch and

s t r e t c h!"

TEN, NINE, EIGHT . . .
SEVEN, SIX, FIVE . . .

We'll send up a rocket,
And it will be LIVE.

FIVE, FOUR, THREE . . .
It's ready to zoom!

We're counting each second,
And soon it will boom!

Get ready for . . . TWO;
Get ready to go . . .

It's TWO–and it's–ONE!
We're OFF! It's ZERO!

Kit Patrickson

RIDDLE

Four stiff-standers,

Four dilly-danders,

Two lookers,

Two crookers,

And a wig-wag.

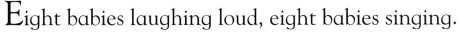

Eight babies laughing loud, eight babies singing.

Seven babies clapping hands, one baby ringing.

Six babies banging drums, two babies rattling.

Five babies dancing high, three babies chattering.

Four babies drinking juice, four babies feeding.

Eight babies ready for bed, eight babies sleeping.

Swinging on a gate, swinging on a gate,
Seven little sisters and a brother makes eight.
Seven pretty pinafores and one bow tie,
Fourteen pigtails and one black eye.

Swinging on a gate, swinging on a gate,
Seven little sisters and a brother makes eight.
Fourteen pretty ribbons and one little cap,
Eight books for school tied up with a strap.

Swinging on a gate, swinging on a gate,
Seven little sisters and a brother makes eight.
The school bell rings, and off they go —
Eight little children all in a row.

Five little monkeys walked along the shore;
One went a-sailing,
Then there were four.

Four little monkeys climbed up a tree;
One of them tumbled down,
Then there were three.

Three little monkeys found a pot of glue;
One got stuck in it,
Then there were two.

Two little monkeys found a currant bun;
One ran away with it,
Then there was one.

One little monkey cried all afternoon,
So they put him in an airplane
And sent him to the moon.

SIX APPLES

Six little apples
hanging on a tree.
Johnny had a big stone
and down came three.

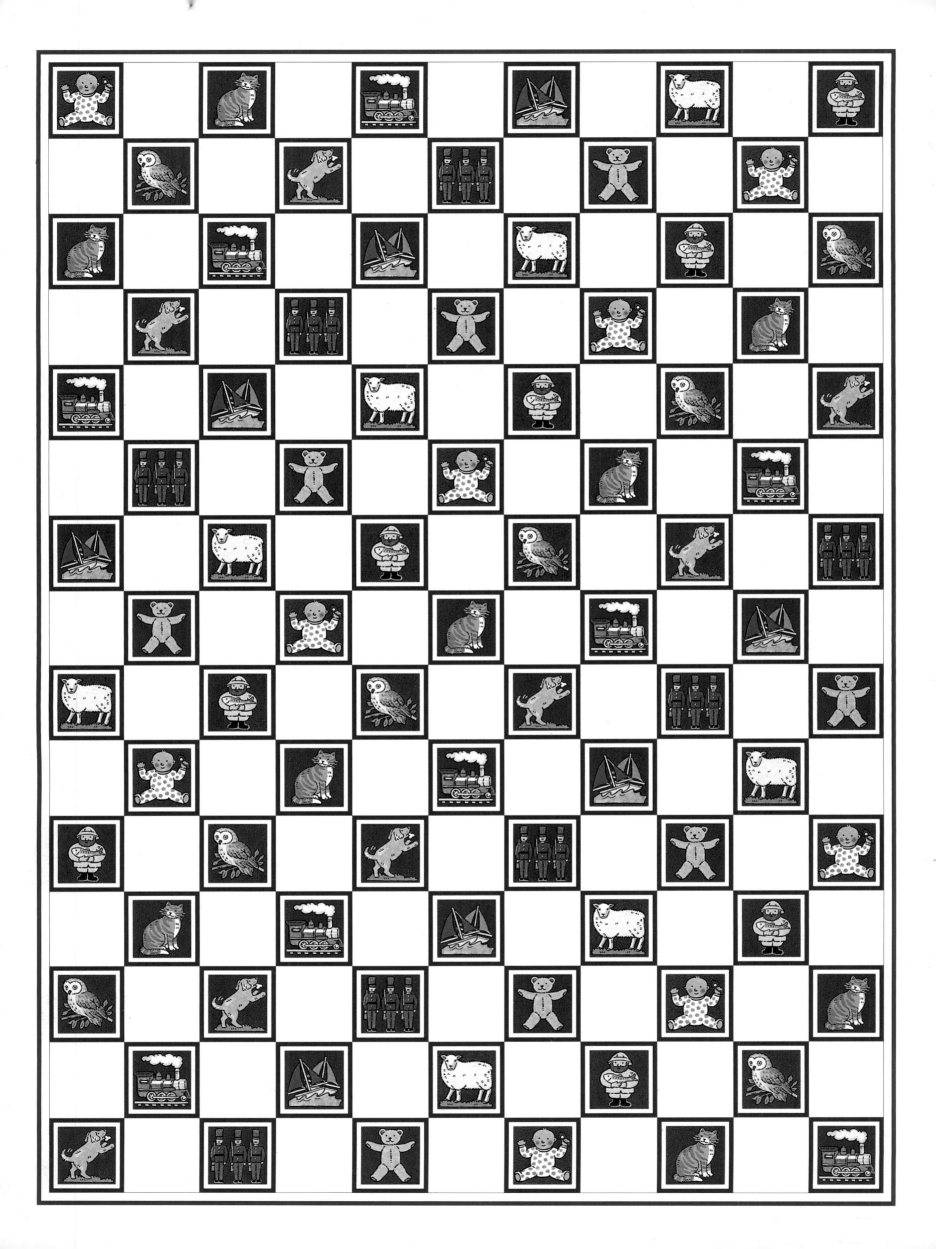